*Cherished Thoughts...*

# *Prayer* on

Zondervan*Gifts*

*We have a gift for inspiration*™

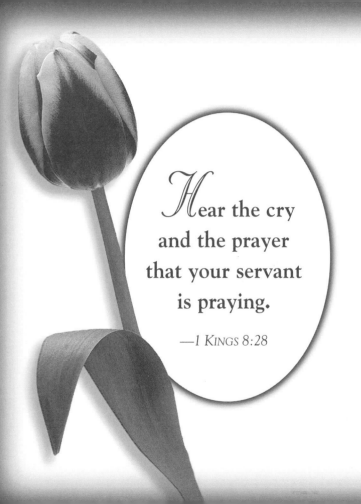

$\mathscr{H}$ear the cry
and the prayer
that your servant
is praying.

—1 KINGS 8:28

*I*n the morning, prayer is the key that opens to us the treasures of God's mercies and blessings; in the evening, it is the key that shuts us up under his protection and safeguard.

—ANONYMOUS

$\mathcal{T}$he LORD said to [Solomon]:
"I have heard the prayer and plea
you have made before me."

—*1 KINGS 9:3*

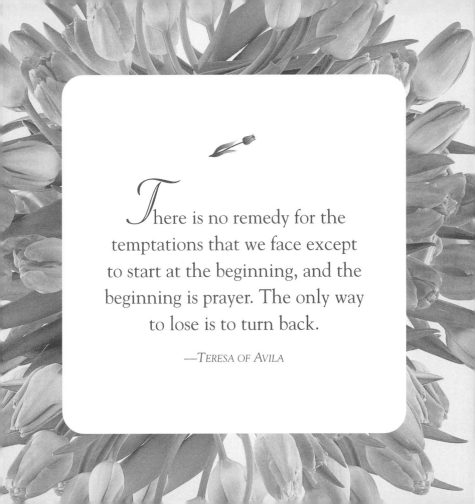

*T*here is no remedy for the temptations that we face except to start at the beginning, and the beginning is prayer. The only way to lose is to turn back.

—TERESA OF AVILA

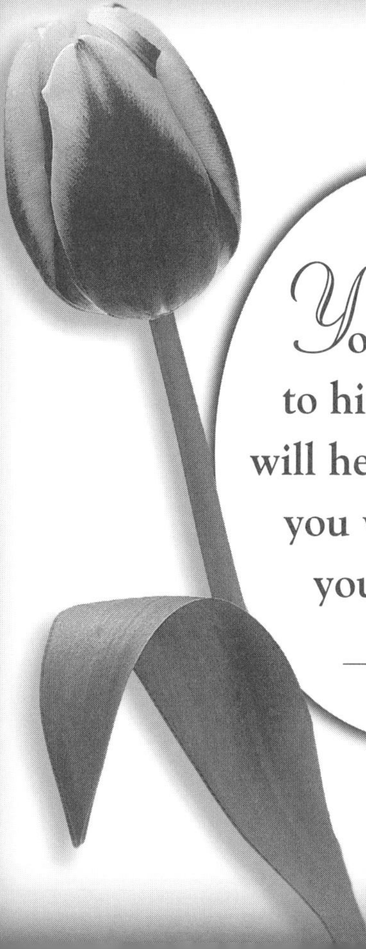

$\mathcal{Y}$ou will pray
to him, and he
will hear you, and
you will fulfill
your vows.

—JOB 22:27

$O$ur prayers must mean something to us if they are to mean anything to God.

—MALTBIE D. BABCOCK

$\mathcal{I}$f you are swept off your feet,
it is time to get on your knees.

—*Fred Beck*

$\mathcal{S}$even days without prayer
makes one weak.

—ALLEN E. BARTLETT

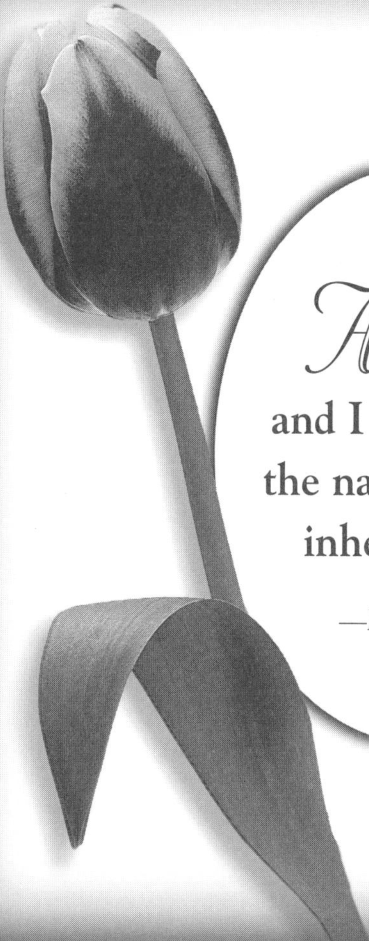

$\mathcal{A}$sk of me,
and I will make
the nations your
inheritance.

—PSALM 2:8

$\mathcal{P}$rayer is the whole of a man's life. There is no thought, feeling, yearning, or desire, however low, trifling, or vulgar we may deem it, which, if it affects our real interest or happiness, we may not lay before God and be sure of sympathy.

—HENRY WARD BEECHER

Answer me when I call to you,
O my righteous God. Give me
relief from my distress; be merciful
to me and hear my prayer.

—PSALM 4:1

He who ceases to pray
ceases to prosper.

—Sir William Gurney Benham

*I*n the
morning, O LORD,
you hear my voice...
I lay my requests
before you and wait
in expectation.

—*PSALM 5:3*

*N*o prayer is lost. Praying breath was never spent in vain. There is no such thing as prayer unanswered or unnoticed by God, and some things that we count refusals or denials are simply delays.

—H. BONAR

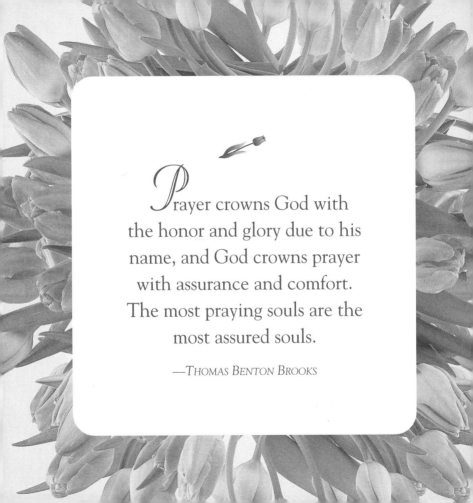

*P*rayer crowns God with the honor and glory due to his name, and God crowns prayer with assurance and comfort. The most praying souls are the most assured souls.

—THOMAS BENTON BROOKS

$\mathcal{G}$od answers sharp and sudden
on some prayers,
And thrusts the thing we have
prayed for in our face,
A gauntlet with a gift in 't.

—ELIZABETH BARRETT BROWNING

The LORD
has heard my cry
for mercy; the LORD
accepts my prayer.

—PSALM 6:9

*I*t matters little what form of prayer we adopt or how many words we use, what matters is the faith which lays hold on God and touches the heart of the Father who knew us long before we came to him.

—DIETRICH BONHOEFFER

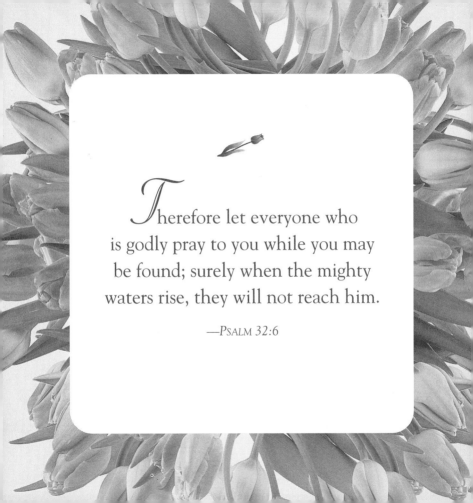

*T*herefore let everyone who
is godly pray to you while you may
be found; surely when the mighty
waters rise, they will not reach him.

—PSALM 32:6

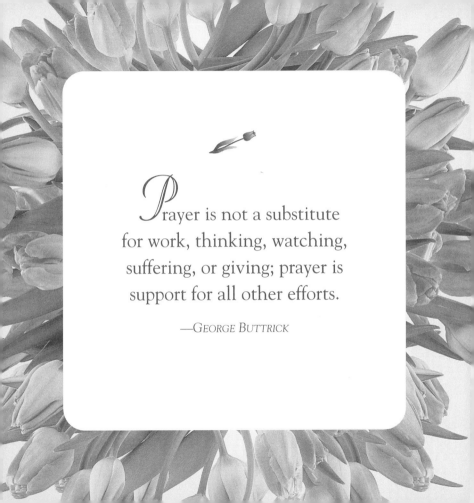

*P*rayer is not a substitute for work, thinking, watching, suffering, or giving; prayer is support for all other efforts.

—GEORGE BUTTRICK

At night his
song is with me—
a prayer to the
God of my life.

—PSALM 42:8

*N*ever will a man pray as he ought unless the Master will guide both his mouth and heart.

—John Calvin

*O* you who hear prayer, to you
all men will come.

—*Psalm 65:2*

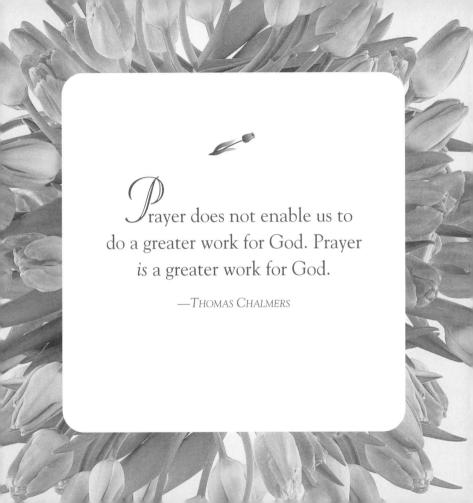

*P*rayer does not enable us to
do a greater work for God. Prayer
*is* a greater work for God.

—THOMAS CHALMERS

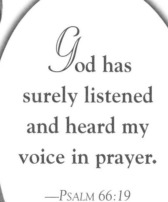

$\mathcal{G}$od has
surely listened
and heard my
voice in prayer.

—PSALM 66:19

$S$tep softly, under snow or rain,
To find the place where men can pray;
The way is all so very plain
That we may lose the way.

—G. K. CHESTERTON

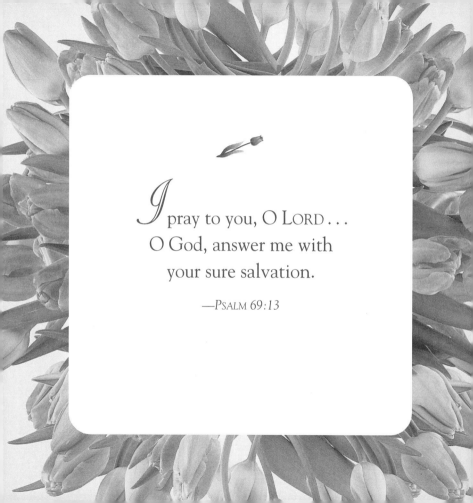

$\mathcal{I}$ pray to you, O LORD . . .
O God, answer me with
your sure salvation.

—PSALM 69:13

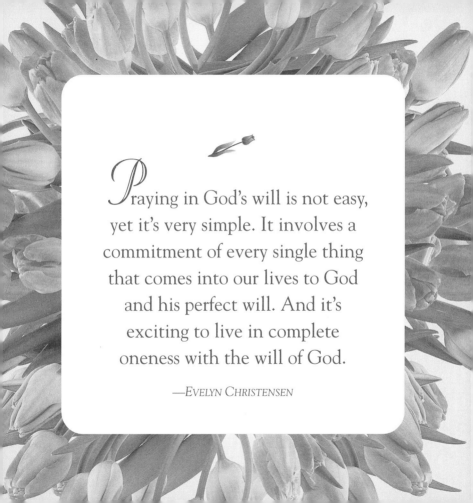

$\mathscr{P}$raying in God's will is not easy, yet it's very simple. It involves a commitment of every single thing that comes into our lives to God and his perfect will. And it's exciting to live in complete oneness with the will of God.

—*Evelyn Christensen*

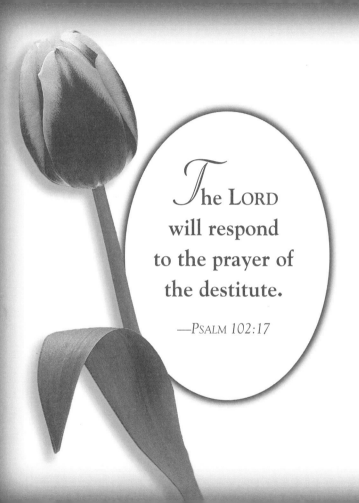

The LORD
will respond
to the prayer of
the destitute.

—*Psalm 102:17*

He prayeth best, who loveth best,
All things both great and small;
For the dear God who loveth us,
He made and loveth all.

—Samuel Taylor Coleridge

_T_he LORD is far from the
wicked but he hears the
prayer of the righteous.

—PROVERBS 15:29

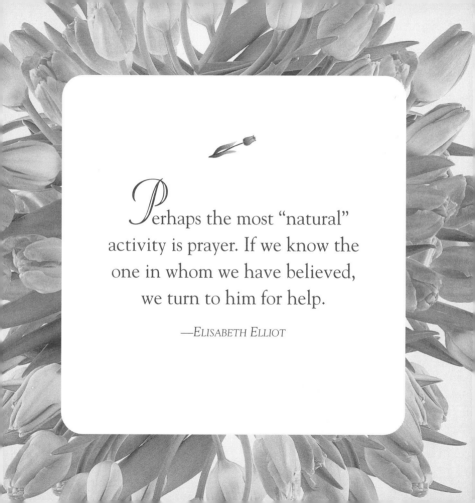

$\mathcal{P}$erhaps the most "natural" activity is prayer. If we know the one in whom we have believed, we turn to him for help.

—ELISABETH ELLIOT

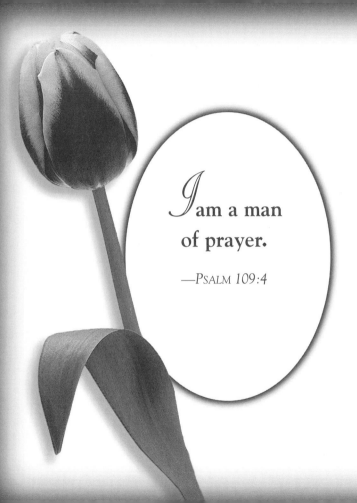

$\mathcal{I}$am a man
of prayer.

—PSALM 109:4

$\mathcal{E}$very time you pray, if your prayer is sincere, there will be new feeling and new meaning in it which will give you fresh courage, and you will understand that prayer is an education.

—FYODOR DOSTOYEVSKY

*M*y prayer is . . . against the
deeds of evildoers.

—*PSALM 141:5*

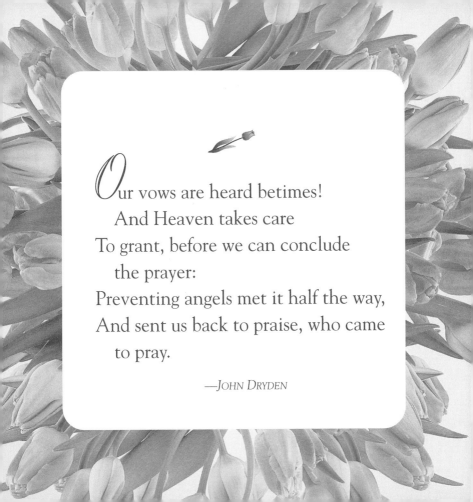

$\mathcal{O}$ur vows are heard betimes!
 And Heaven takes care
To grant, before we can conclude
 the prayer:
Preventing angels met it half the way,
And sent us back to praise, who came
 to pray.

—JOHN DRYDEN

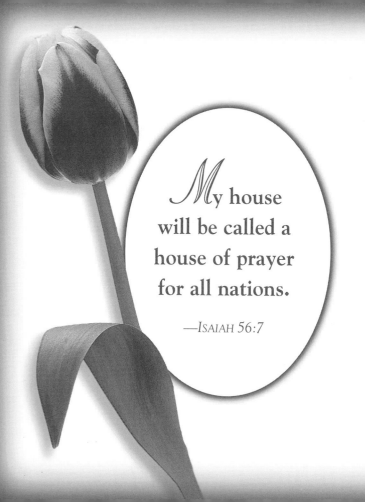

*M*y house
will be called a
house of prayer
for all nations.

—*Isaiah* 56:7

All of prayer is a relationship with God, and "asking prayer" is a special part of that relationship. Often it is the first step in our relationship with God. As we tell God about our needs, and listen to him answer us—our relationship with him grows.

—COLLEEN TOWNSEND EVANS

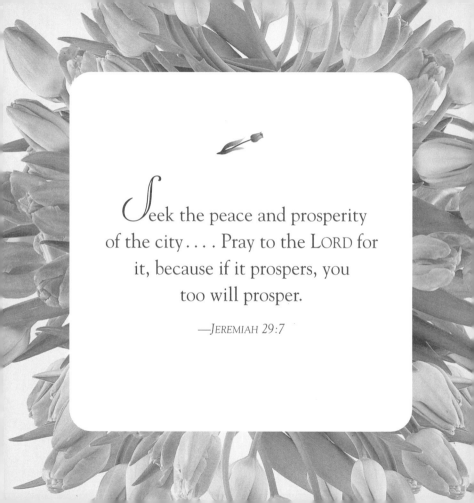

$\mathcal{S}$eek the peace and prosperity
of the city. . . . Pray to the LORD for
it, because if it prospers, you
too will prosper.

—JEREMIAH 29:7

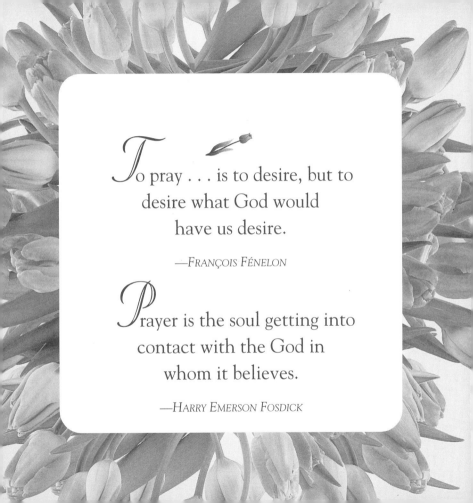

*T*o pray . . . is to desire, but to
desire what God would
have us desire.

—François Fénelon

*P*rayer is the soul getting into
contact with the God in
whom it believes.

—Harry Emerson Fosdick

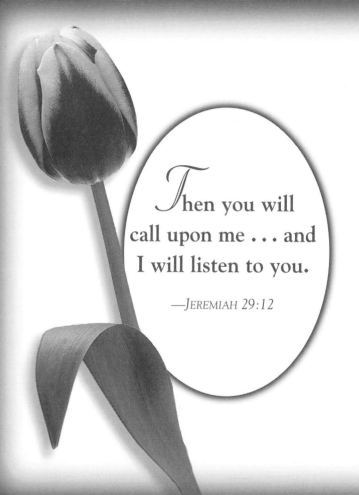

*T*hen you will
call upon me . . . and
I will listen to you.

—JEREMIAH 29:12

*W*ork as if you were to live a hundred years. Pray as if you were to die tomorrow.

—BENJAMIN FRANKLIN

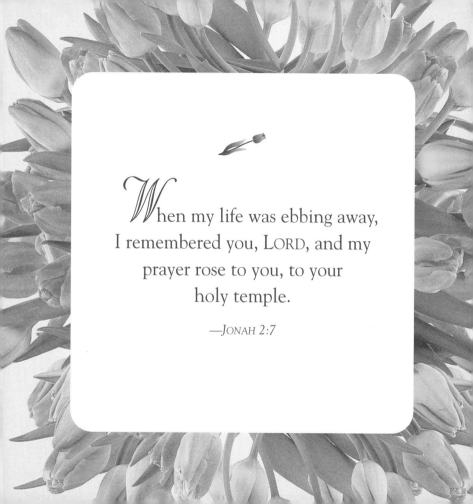

When my life was ebbing away,
I remembered you, LORD, and my
prayer rose to you, to your
holy temple.

—JONAH 2:7

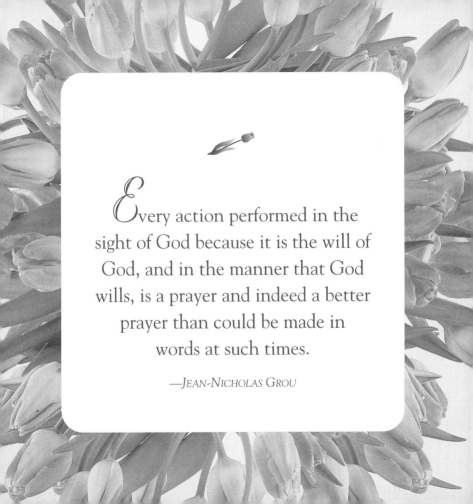

*E*very action performed in the sight of God because it is the will of God, and in the manner that God wills, is a prayer and indeed a better prayer than could be made in words at such times.

—JEAN-NICHOLAS GROU

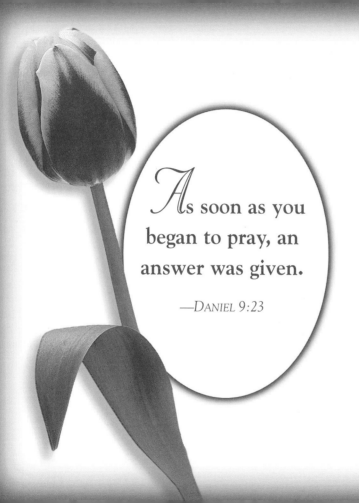

As soon as you began to pray, an answer was given.

—DANIEL 9:23

$\mathcal{T}$he Spirit . . . is the Master Pray-er. He knows God's will perfectly. He knows what best to be praying under all circumstances. And he is within you and me.

—S. D. GORDON

*L*ove your enemies and pray for
those who persecute you.

—MATTHEW 5:44

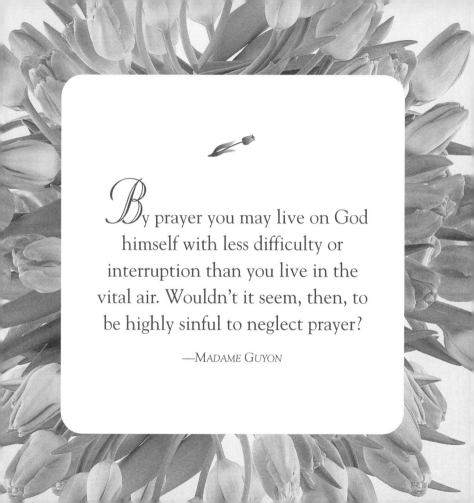

By prayer you may live on God himself with less difficulty or interruption than you live in the vital air. Wouldn't it seem, then, to be highly sinful to neglect prayer?

—MADAME GUYON

*W*hen you pray, go into your room, close the door and pray to your Father, who is unseen.

—MATTHEW 6:6

*I*t is good for us to keep some account of our prayers, that we may not unsay them in our practice.

—MATTHEW HENRY

*W*ho goes to bed
   and does not pray,
Maketh two nights
   to every day.

—GEORGE HERBERT

$\mathcal{Y}$our Father knows what you
need before you ask him.

—MATTHEW 6:8

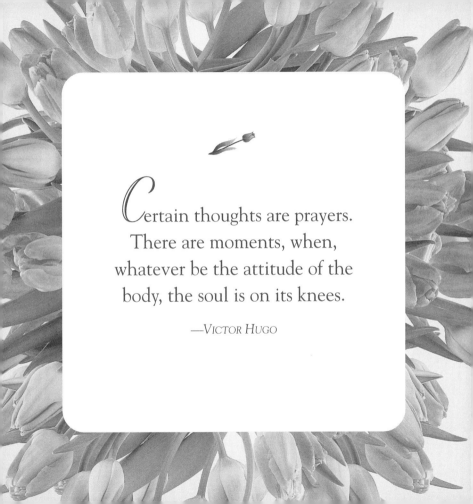

$\mathscr{C}$ertain thoughts are prayers.
There are moments, when,
whatever be the attitude of the
body, the soul is on its knees.

—VICTOR HUGO

Ask and
it will be given
to you.

—MATTHEW 7:7

$\mathcal{A}$n intercessor means one who is in such vital contact with God and with people that he is like a live wire closing the gap between the saving power of God and the sinful men who have been cut off from that power.

—HANNAH HURNARD

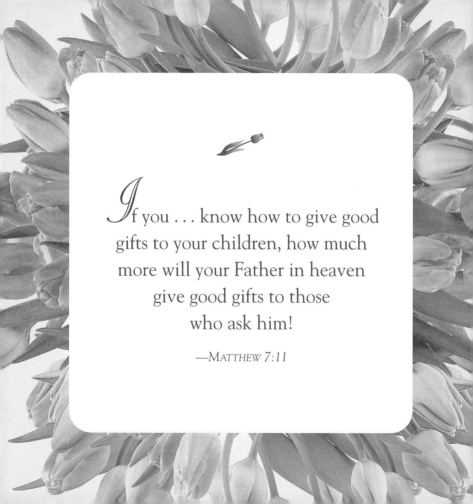

*I*f you . . . know how to give good
gifts to your children, how much
more will your Father in heaven
give good gifts to those
who ask him!

—MATTHEW 7:11

$\mathcal{P}$rayer not only changes
situations, things, and people. It
also changes those who pray.

—PATRICK JOHNSTONE

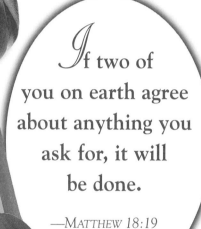

*If* two of
you on earth agree
about anything you
ask for, it will
be done.

—Matthew 18:19

$\mathcal{A}$nd help us, this and every day,
To live more nearly as we pray.

—JOHN KEBLE

$\mathcal{P}$rayer is exhaling the spirit of man
and inhaling the spirit
of God.

—EDWIN KEITH

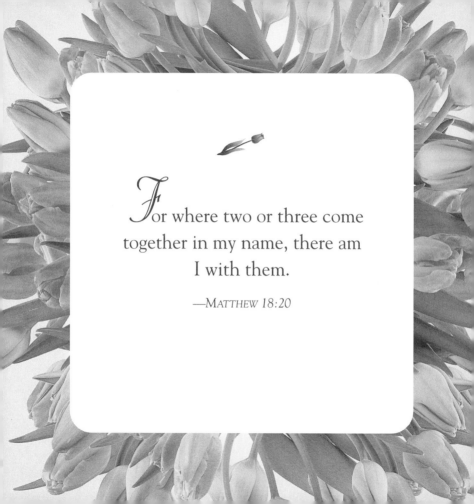

*F*or where two or three come
together in my name, there am
I with them.

—MATTHEW 18:20

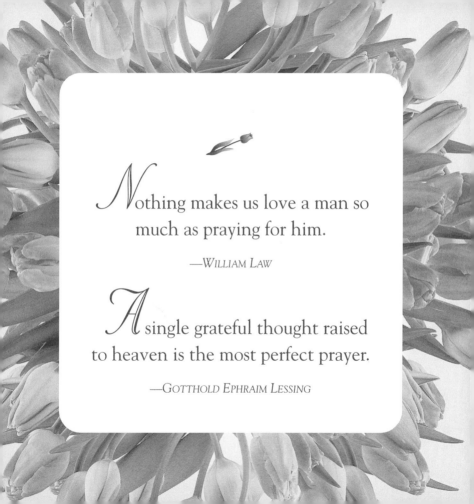

*N*othing makes us love a man so
much as praying for him.

—WILLIAM LAW

*A* single grateful thought raised
to heaven is the most perfect prayer.

—GOTTHOLD EPHRAIM LESSING

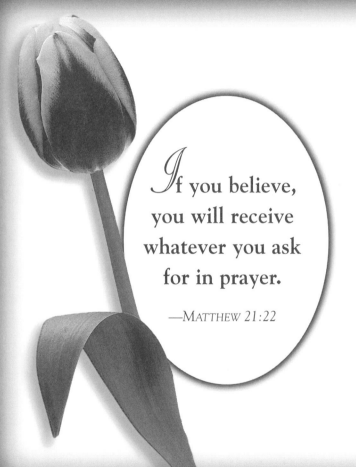

*If* you believe,
you will receive
whatever you ask
for in prayer.

—MATTHEW 21:22

$\mathscr{F}$or me, prayer is an upward leap of the heart, an untroubled glance toward heaven, a cry of gratitude and love which I utter from the depths of sorrow as well as from the heights of joy.

—*THÉRÈSE OF LISIEUX*

Watch and pray so that you will not fall into temptation. The spirit is willing, but the body is weak.

—MATTHEW 26:41

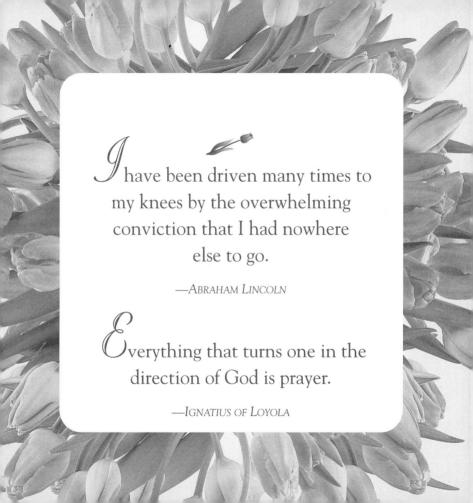

*I* have been driven many times to my knees by the overwhelming conviction that I had nowhere else to go.

—ABRAHAM LINCOLN

*E*verything that turns one in the direction of God is prayer.

—IGNATIUS OF LOYOLA

$\mathcal{B}$less those
who curse you,
pray for those who
mistreat you.

—*LUKE 6:28*

$\mathcal{N}$one can believe how powerful prayer is, and what it is able to effect, but those who have learned it by experience.

—MARTIN LUTHER

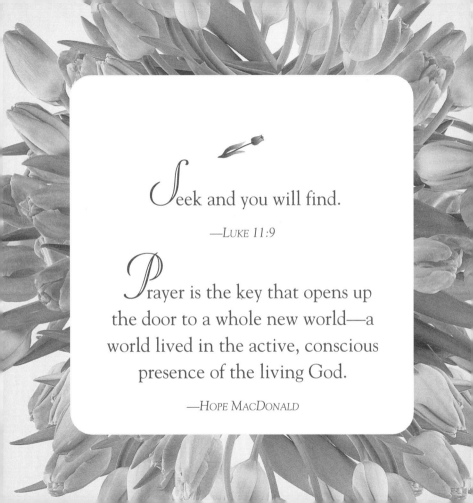

*S*eek and you will find.

—*Luke 11:9*

*P*rayer is the key that opens up
the door to a whole new world—a
world lived in the active, conscious
presence of the living God.

—Hope MacDonald

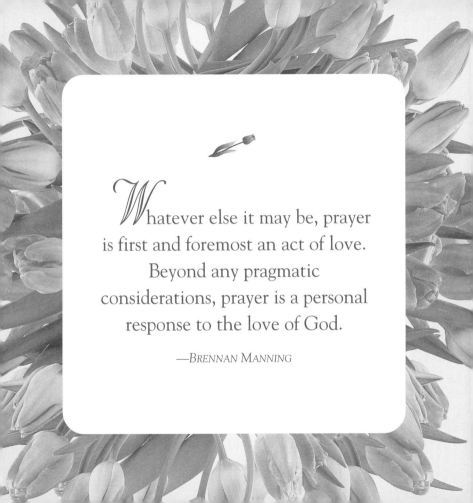

Whatever else it may be, prayer is first and foremost an act of love. Beyond any pragmatic considerations, prayer is a personal response to the love of God.

—BRENNAN MANNING

To him who knocks, the door will be opened.

—LUKE 11:10

$\mathcal{I}$t is . . . dangerous business to pray for something unless you really and truly mean it. You see, God might call your bluff, take you up on it . . . and would you be surprised!

—PETER MARSHALL

*J*esus told his disciples a parable to show them that they should always pray and not give up.

—*LUKE 18:1*

*P*rayer was never meant to be incidental to the work of God. It *is* the work.

—*ARTHUR MATHEWS*

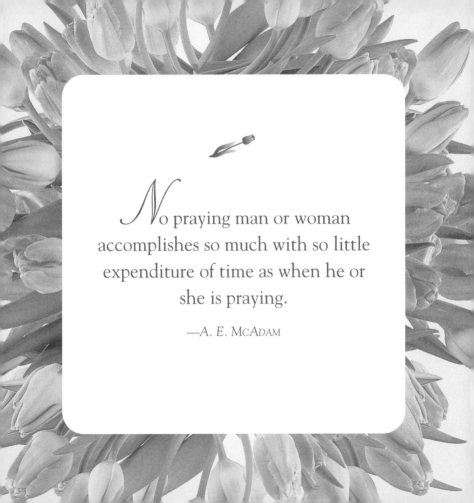

*N*o praying man or woman accomplishes so much with so little expenditure of time as when he or she is praying.

—A. E. MCADAM

*I*f you remain in me and my words remain in you, ask whatever you wish, and it will be given you.

—John 15:7

*P*rayer is love raised to its greatest power; and the prayer of intercession is the noblest and most Christian kind of prayer because in it love—and imagination—reach their highest and widest range.

—ROBERT J. MCCRACKEN

*A*sk and you will receive, and
your joy will be complete.

—JOHN 16:24

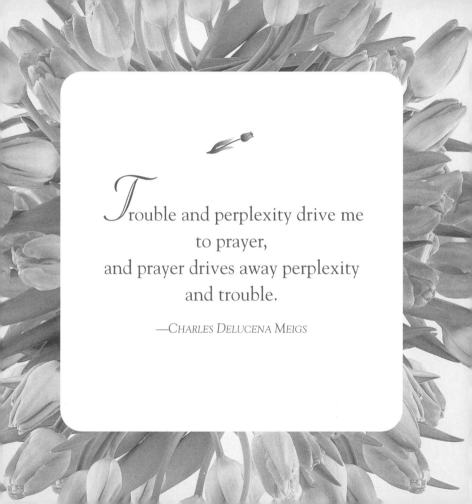

$\mathcal{T}$rouble and perplexity drive me
to prayer,
and prayer drives away perplexity
and trouble.

—CHARLES DELUCENA MEIGS

$\mathcal{W}$e do not know what we ought to pray for, but the Spirit himself intercedes for us.

—ROMANS 8:26

*P*rayer and love are learned in the hour when prayer has become impossible and your heart has turned to stone.

—THOMAS MERTON

𝓑e joyful in hope, patient in affliction, faithful in prayer.

—ROMANS 12:12

Prayer is the soul's sincere desire,
 Uttered or unexpressed;
The motion of a hidden fire
That trembles in the breast.

—JAMES MONTGOMERY

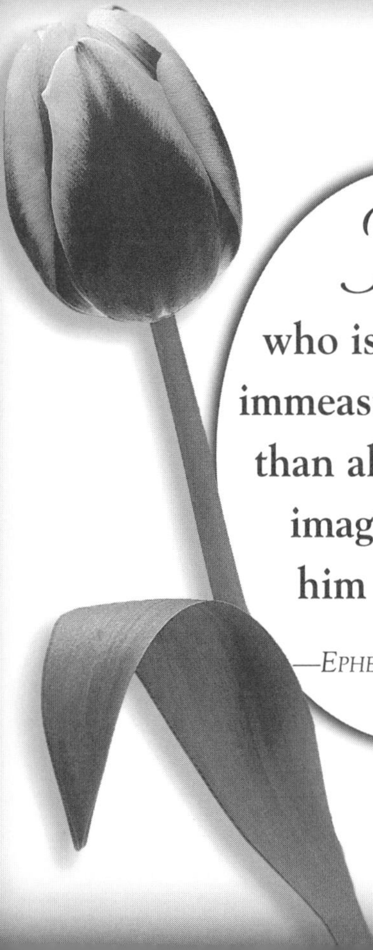

*T*o him
who is able to do
immeasurably more
than all we ask or
imagine . . . to
him be glory.

—*Ephesians 3:20–21*

*P*rayer is not eloquence, but earnestness; not the definition of helplessness, but the feeling of it; not figures of speech, but earnestness of soul.

—HANNAH MORE

$\mathscr{P}$ray in the Spirit on all
occasions with all kinds of
prayers and requests.

—EPHESIANS 6:18

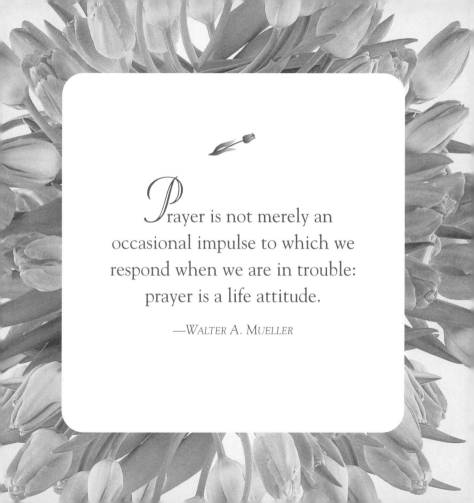

$\mathcal{P}$rayer is not merely an occasional impulse to which we respond when we are in trouble: prayer is a life attitude.

—WALTER A. MUELLER

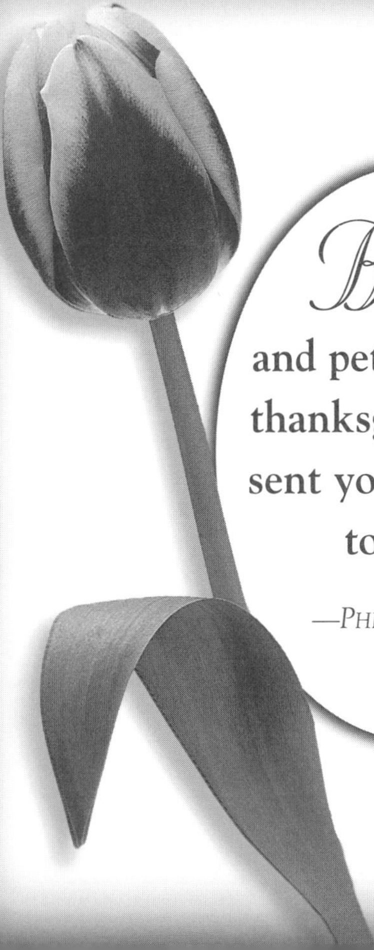

$\mathcal{B}$y prayer
and petition, with
thanksgiving, pre-
sent your requests
to God.

—Philippians 4:6

*N*ow I lay me down to sleep,

I pray the Lord my soul to keep;

If I should die before I wake,

I pray the Lord my soul to take.

—THE NEW ENGLAND PRIMER

$\mathcal{D}$evote yourselves to prayer,
being watchful and thankful.

—COLOSSIANS 4:2

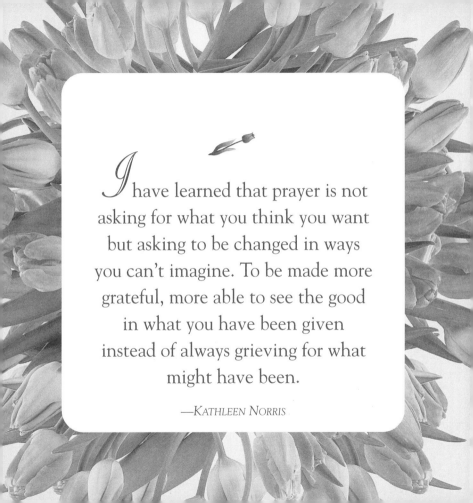

*I* have learned that prayer is not asking for what you think you want but asking to be changed in ways you can't imagine. To be made more grateful, more able to see the good in what you have been given instead of always grieving for what might have been.

—KATHLEEN NORRIS

*P*ray
**continually.**

—*1 Thessalonians 5:17*

*A* sinning man will stop praying. A praying man will stop sinning.

—LEONARD RAVENHILL

*P*ray for us that the message of
the Lord may spread rapidly
and be honored.

—*2 Thessalonians 3:1*

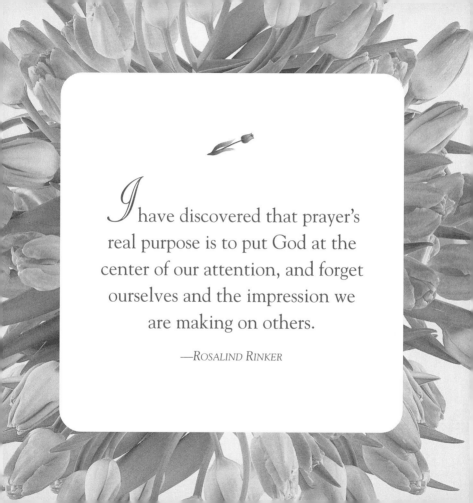

*I* have discovered that prayer's real purpose is to put God at the center of our attention, and forget ourselves and the impression we are making on others.

—ROSALIND RINKER

*L*ift up holy
hands in prayer,
without anger or
disputing.

—*1 Timothy 2:8*

$\mathcal{W}$e are the womb of God upon the earth. We are not the source of life, but we are carriers of the source of life. We do not generate life, but we release, through prayer, him who does.

—DUTCH SHEETS

*I* pray that you may be active in sharing your faith, so that you will have a full understanding of every good thing we have in Christ.

—*Philemon 6*

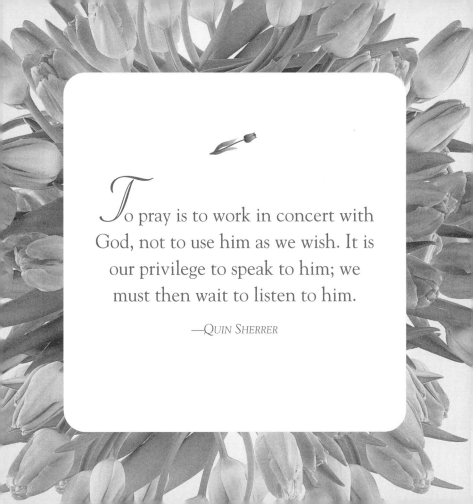

$\mathcal{T}$o pray is to work in concert with God, not to use him as we wish. It is our privilege to speak to him; we must then wait to listen to him.

—QUIN SHERRER

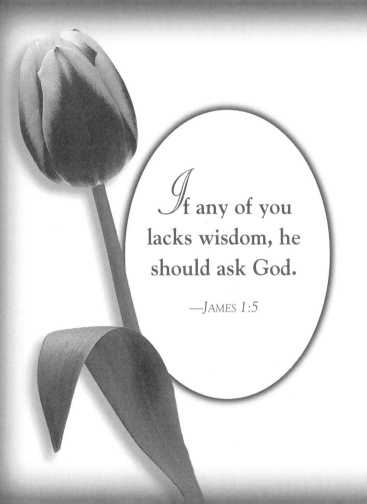

*I*f any of you
lacks wisdom, he
should ask God.

—JAMES 1:5

"*If* ye abide in me, and my words abide in you." Here are the two feet by which we climb to power with God in prayer.

—CHARLES SPURGEON

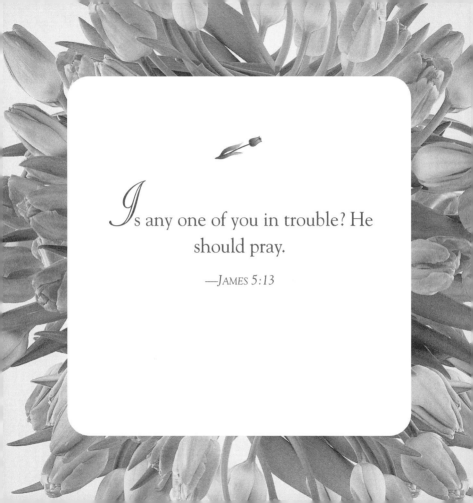

$\mathcal{I}$s any one of you in trouble? He should pray.

—JAMES 5:13

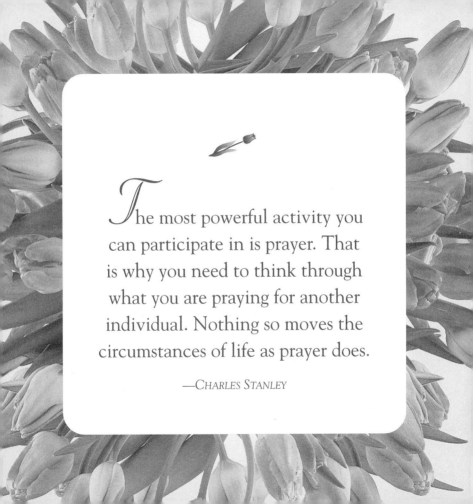

$\mathcal{T}$he most powerful activity you can participate in is prayer. That is why you need to think through what you are praying for another individual. Nothing so moves the circumstances of life as prayer does.

—CHARLES STANLEY

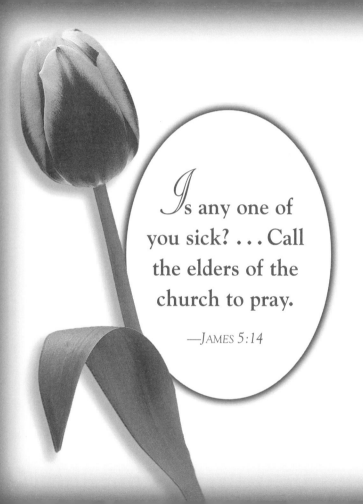

*I*s any one of
you sick? . . . Call
the elders of the
church to pray.

—JAMES 5:14

$\mathcal{P}$rayer is the peace of our spirit, the stillness of our thoughts, the evenness of our recollection, the sea of our meditation, the rest of our cares, and the calm of our tempest.

—*JEREMY TAYLOR*

The prayer of a righteous man is
powerful and effective.

—JAMES 5:16

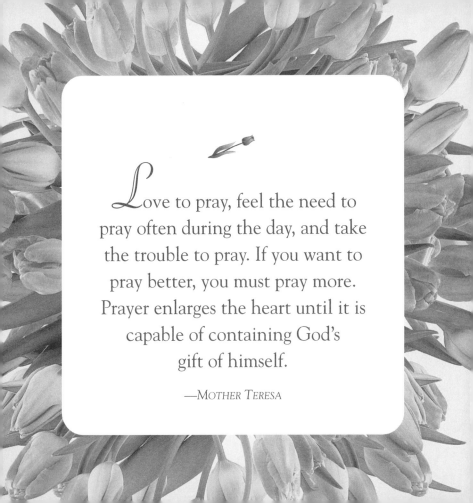

$\mathcal{L}$ove to pray, feel the need to pray often during the day, and take the trouble to pray. If you want to pray better, you must pray more. Prayer enlarges the heart until it is capable of containing God's gift of himself.

—MOTHER TERESA

$\mathcal{B}$e clear minded and self-controlled so that you can pray.

—1 PETER 4:7

Oh, the power of prayer to reach down, down, down where hope itself seems vain, and lift men and women up, up, up into fellowship with and likeness to God.

—R. A. Torrey

$\mathscr{I}$f our hearts do not condemn us,
we have confidence before God and
receive from him anything we ask.

—1 JOHN 3:21–22

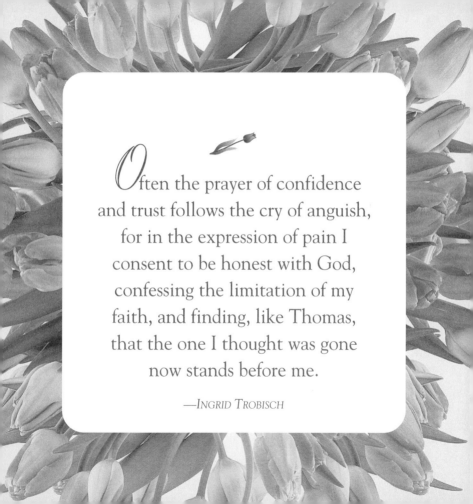

$O$ften the prayer of confidence
and trust follows the cry of anguish,
for in the expression of pain I
consent to be honest with God,
confessing the limitation of my
faith, and finding, like Thomas,
that the one I thought was gone
now stands before me.

—INGRID TROBISCH

*I*f we ask any-
thing according
to his will, he
hears us.

—1 John 5:14

$\mathscr{W}$hatever a man prays for, he prays for a miracle.

—IVAN SERGEYEVICH TURGENEV

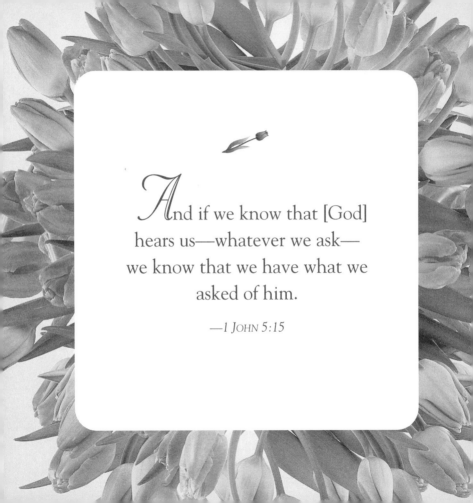

*A*nd if we know that [God] hears us—whatever we ask— we know that we have what we asked of him.

—*1 John 5:15*

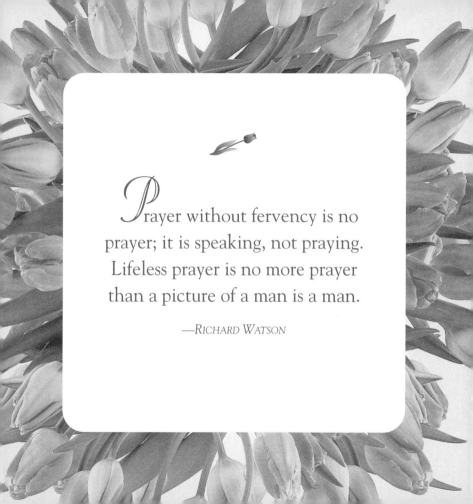

*P*rayer without fervency is no prayer; it is speaking, not praying. Lifeless prayer is no more prayer than a picture of a man is a man.

—RICHARD WATSON

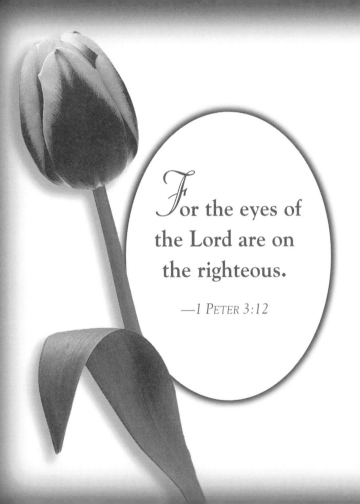

$\mathcal{F}$or the eyes of
the Lord are on
the righteous.

—1 PETER 3:12

$\mathcal{E}$very chain that spirits wear
Crumbles in the breath of prayer.

—JOHN GREENLEAF WHITTIER

$\mathcal{B}$uild yourselves up in your
most holy faith and pray in
the Holy Spirit.

—JUDE 20

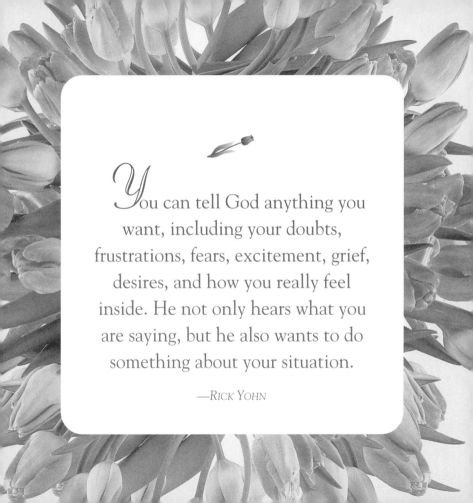

$\mathcal{Y}$ou can tell God anything you want, including your doubts, frustrations, fears, excitement, grief, desires, and how you really feel inside. He not only hears what you are saying, but he also wants to do something about your situation.

—RICK YOHN

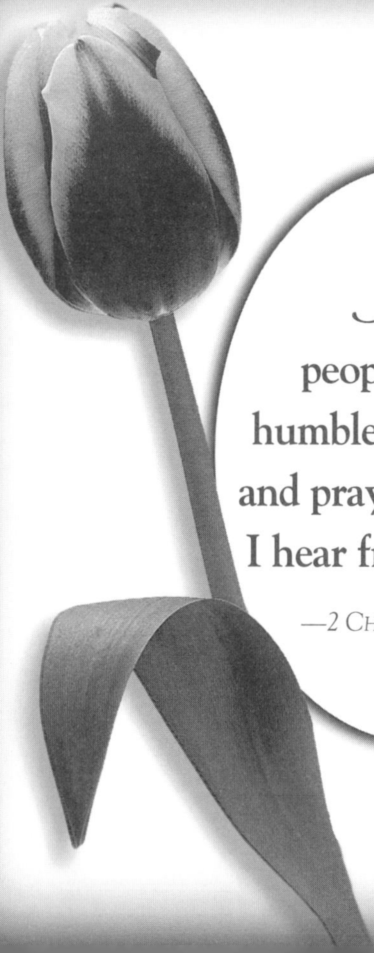

*I*f my
people ... will
humble themselves
and pray ... then will
I hear from heaven.

—2 CHRONICLES 7:14

$\mathcal{P}$rayer is the lifting up of the heart to God.

—JOHN WESLEY

*P*rayer begins by thinking of God
earnestly and humbly to the
exclusion of other objects
of thought.

—EVELYN UNDERHILL

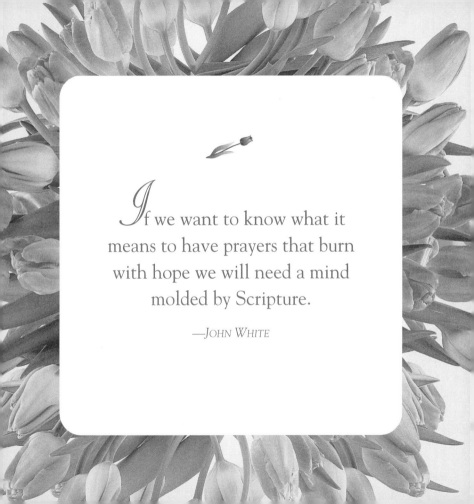

If we want to know what it means to have prayers that burn with hope we will need a mind molded by Scripture.

—JOHN WHITE

$\mathcal{I}$will spread out my hands in prayer to the LORD.

—*Exodus* 9:29

$\mathcal{P}$rayer will increase in power and reality as we repudiate all pretense and learn to be utterly honest before God as well as before men.

—A. W. TOZER

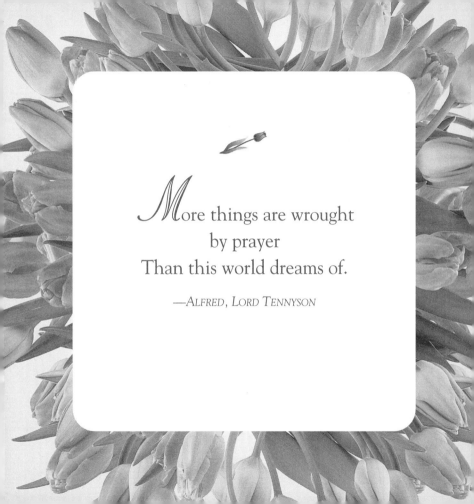

$\mathscr{M}$ore things are wrought
by prayer
Than this world dreams of.

—ALFRED, LORD TENNYSON

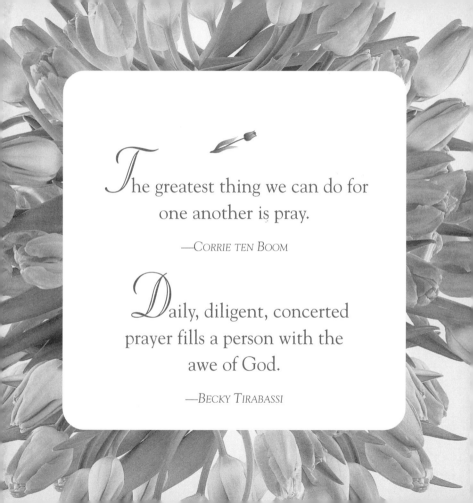

*T*he greatest thing we can do for one another is pray.

—CORRIE TEN BOOM

*D*aily, diligent, concerted prayer fills a person with the awe of God.

—BECKY TIRABASSI

*T*his is what
I seek: . . . to gaze
upon the beauty of
the LORD and to seek
him in his temple.

—PSALM 27:4